AF370616

s its lu

tion an
life to

pts you

istead,

multidi

healing

onal ar
it has a

healing,
life I h

join m

m

nd my
lspring
s throu

my app
siding

and tra

idation

ımmin
ɔf dark

g Love

ected w
ɔr of all

embrac

repres
culine

ich sig
ing th

vhat is 1
reveal t

world, 1

hey see1

nly by
lf and

es, ider
usly un

ever, it
d we a
1

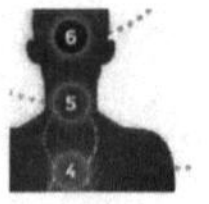

practi

have ou
shapes

in speech (s

CHAKR

the 4th chak

s, we ga

s.

tions.

me not
hat al

:s and

," whicl

e, love,
ies fore

onal frequ
sciousness
s. As huma
s of consc

orning,

nd high
ir energ
r

e.

ise tea

ty is sor

by hov

ie creat

se desir

ɔ make
ıt pain.

ess, we

can be s
dance.

true se.

; what

child i
happy

it pract

:oo late
caressi

ns that

body w

mold, b

1

cation k
ı as the '

body.

ncing

allowii
trauma

out a st

progr

ns and

s. Love

1 and t

anges.

ldress a
s within

ower t(

7e are

--

ew indi

existenc

ociated

possibil

are   e

s can tr

change

. by m

a progr

. Delve